The Heinemann Illustrated Encyclopedia

Volume 7

New-Pra

First published in Great Britain by Heinemann Library
Halley Court, Jordan Hill, Oxford OX2 8EJ
a division of Reed Educational and Professional Publishing Ltd.

OXFORD MELBOURNE AUCKLAND
JOHANNESBURG BLANTYRE GABORONE
IBADAN PORTSMOUTH NH (USA) CHICAGO

Series Editors: Rebecca and Stephen Vickers
Author Team: Rob Alcraft, Catherine Chambers, Jim Drake,
Fred Martin, Angela Royston, Jane Shuter, Roger Thomas,
Rebecca Vickers, Stephen Vickers
Reading Consultant: Betty Root

Photo research by Katharine Smith
Designed and Typeset by Gecko Ltd
Printed in Hong Kong by Wing King Tong

02 01 00 99 98
10 9 8 7 6 5 4 3 2 1

ISBN 0 431 09058 0

British Library Cataloguing in Publication Data.

The Heinemann illustrated encyclopedia
   1. Children's encyclopedias and dictionaries
   I. Vickers, Rebecca II. Vickers, Stephen, 1951–
032

ISBN 0431090629

Acknowledgements:
Cover: The cover illustration is of a male specimen of *Ornithoptera goliath*, commonly called the
Goliath Birdwing. Special thanks to Dr George C. McGavin and the Hope Entomological
Collections, Oxford University Museum of Natural History.

J. Allan Cash Ltd: pp4, 5, 6, 8, 9, 10, 16, 23b, 24, 25, 27, 32, 42, 47. **Ancient Art and Architecture:** p15.
Ardea London Ltd: D. Parer and E. Parer-Cook – p40b. **BBC Music Live:** Henrietta Butler – p18.
Bridgeman Art Library: p23t. **Trevor Clifford Photography:** p39. **Empics:** p11. **The Hutchison
Library:** Robert Francis – p33; Bernard Gerard – p31b. **Oxford Scientific Film:** p13; Doug Allen –
p29b; Kathie Atkinson – p36; G.I. Bernard – p35t; Tony Bomford – p22t; Stanley Breeden – p28b;
Neil Bromaic – p17b; Daniel Cox – 21b; Tim Davies – p19; Rudie Kuper – p14b; Dr Richard k. La Val
– p28t; Lon Lauber – p20b; Tom and Pat Leeson – p45b; Tom McHugh – p40t; Richard Packwood –
p43r; Kjell Sandved – pp26b, 29t; H. Schwind – p35b; Keren Su – p26t; Tom Ulrich – p17t; Vanessa Vick
– p43l; Norbert Wu – p14t. **Performing Arts Library:** p16t. **Popperfoto:** p41. **Redferns:** Chris
Blackwell – p31t; Grant Davis – p44b; David Redfern – p44t. **RSPCA Photo Library:** John George –
p20t. **Science Photo Library:** pp30b, 37. **Still Pictures:** Michael Gunther – p7. **Tony Stone
Worldwide:** Chad Ehlers – p30t. **Trip:** H. Rogers – p22b. **Zefa:** Thomas Braise – p46.

Welcome to the
Heinemann Illustrated Encyclopedia

What is an encyclopedia?

An encyclopedia is an information book. It gives the most important facts about a lot of different subjects. This encyclopedia has been specially written for children your age. It covers many of the subjects from school and others you may find interesting.

What is in this encyclopedia?

In this encyclopedia each topic is called an entry. There is one page for every entry. The entries in this encyclopedia are on:

- animals
- plants
- dinosaurs
- countries
- geography
- history
- world religions
- music
- art
- transport
- science
- technology

How to use this encyclopedia

This encyclopedia has eleven books, called volumes. The first ten volumes contain entries. The entries are all in alphabetical order. This means that Volume One starts with entries that begin with the letter 'A' and Volume Ten ends with entries that begin with the letter 'Z'. Volume Eleven is the index volume and has some other interesting information in its Fact Finder section.

Here are two entries, showing you what you can find on a page:

The See also *line* tells you where to find other related information.

This is the letter that the entry starts with.

Fact boxes give you details about the topic.

Did You Know? *boxes* have fun or interesting bits of information.

The Fact File tells you important facts and figures.

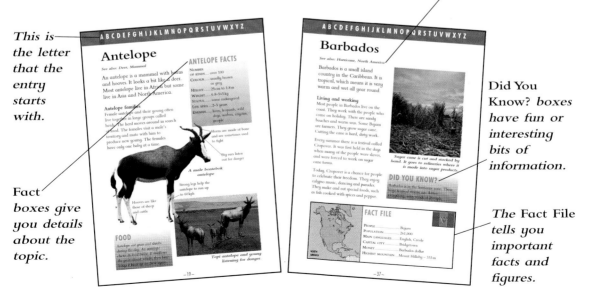

New Zealand

See also: Australasia, Kiwi

New Zealand is a country in the south Pacific Ocean made up of two main islands. Both islands have mountains. North Island has volcanoes and hot springs. South Island has forests, glaciers and lakes.

Living and working

Most people in New Zealand live and work in the cities. There are factories making food products, including butter, to sell to other countries. Farmers grow grains, potatoes, fruit and vegetables. There are large farms for sheep and cattle.

Most New Zealanders are descended from European settlers. The native people of New Zealand are called the Maori. Most of the place names in the country are Maori. Two popular shellfish used in Maori recipes are *toheroa* and *tuatua*.

These Maori women are dancing at a local festival.

DID YOU KNOW?

The national bird of New Zealand is the kiwi, a bird that cannot fly. 'Kiwi' has become the nickname for a New Zealander.

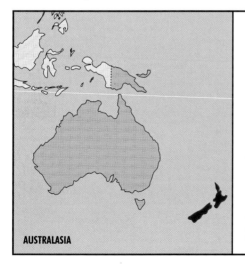

AUSTRALASIA

FACT FILE

PEOPLE.................. New Zealanders

POPULATION.......... 3.5 million

MAIN LANGUAGES.. English, Maori

CAPITAL CITY........ Wellington

BIGGEST CITY........ Auckland

MONEY .... New Zealand dollar

HIGHEST
MOUNTAIN............. Mount Cook – 3753 m

LONGEST RIVER..... Waikato – 435 km

Nicaragua

See also: North America

Nicaragua is a small country in Central America. There are mountains with volcanoes that still erupt. Earthquakes sometimes cause great damage. Along the east coast there is an area of flat land called the Mosquito Coast. There are two very big lakes. There is rainforest where it is wet and grassland where it is drier.

DID YOU KNOW?

There were Native American people living in Nicaragua before Spanish settlers arrived from Europe. The country is named after the Native American chief, Nicara.

Living and working

Most people in Nicaragua work on farms. They grow maize, beans, rice, coffee and cotton. Cattle are raised on big ranches. There is mining for gold and copper.

Tourists visit the beaches and the lakes in the craters of inactive volcanoes. People enjoy lively music and the marimba dance. Favourite foods include corn pancakes, called tortillas, and fried rice with beans.

This is the main road through a village in Jalapa in Nicaragua

NORTH AMERICA

FACT FILE

PEOPLE	Nicaraguans
POPULATION	4.3 million
MAIN LANGUAGE	Spanish
CAPITAL CITY	Managua
MONEY	Gold córdoba
HIGHEST MOUNTAIN	Cerro Mogoton – 2107 m
LONGEST RIVER	Rio Coco – 780 km

Nigeria

See also: Africa

Nigeria is a country in West Africa. The north is hot with grassland. There are rainforests in the south and mountains in the east. The coast has swamps.

Living and working

More people live in Nigeria than in any other country in Africa. Most people live in the countryside. Farmers grow cocoa, grains, cotton, cassava, yams and peanuts. A lot of oil is mined and sold to other countries.

Nigerians come from 250 different tribal groups. There are many languages and customs. In farming areas, harvest festivals are celebrated with special songs and drumming. A favourite food in Nigeria is bean cakes, fried in peanut oil. They are eaten with the vegetable okra and spicy sauces.

In the countryside, cereals such as guinea corn are ground up with a stick and used to make food

DID YOU KNOW?

Abuja is Nigeria's new capital city. It was only finished in 1991. By the year 2000, about one million people will live there.

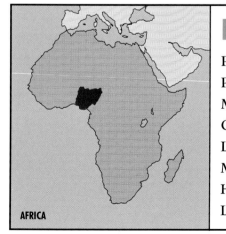

AFRICA

FACT FILE

PEOPLE	Nigerians
POPULATION	88.5 million
MAIN LANGUAGES	English, Hausa, Yoruba, Ibo
CAPITAL CITY	Abuja
LARGEST CITY	Lagos
MONEY	Naira
HIGHEST MOUNTAIN	Dimlang – 2042 m
LONGEST RIVER	Niger-Benue – 1800 km

North America

See also: Continent, Native Americans

North America is the third biggest continent. The Atlantic Ocean is to the east. The Pacific Ocean is to the west. There are eighteen countries in North America.

The land

Most of North America is flat grassy land, called plains. The Rocky Mountains are in the west.

Climate, plants and animals

The coldest places are in the far north. It is hot in the south near the Gulf of Mexico and in the Caribbean Sea. In Mexico and Central America there are deserts, rainforests and grasslands. In the large pine forests in the north there are bears and wolves.

People in North America

The first people to live in North America were the Native Americans. Over time, people from many other countries have come to live there. Now about 360 million people live in North America.

DID YOU KNOW?

Death Valley in the United States is one of the hottest places in the world. Temperatures are sometimes higher than 52°C.

NORTH AMERICA FACTS

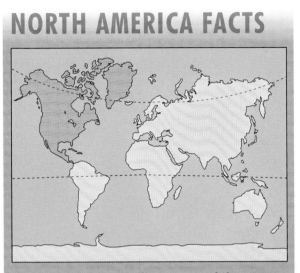

SIZE	24.2 million square kilometres
LARGEST CITY	Mexico City
HIGHEST MOUNTAIN	Mount McKinley – 6194 m
LONGEST RIVER	Mississippi River – 3779 km
SPECIAL FEATURES	the five Great Lakes Niagara Falls

The Niagara Falls are on the border between Canada and the United States.

North Korea

See also: Asia, South Korea

North Korea is a country on the Pacific coast of Asia. There are hills and mountains over most of the land. It is usually very cold in winter. Summer is hot and very wet. Forest covers about three-quarters of the country.

Living and working

Just under half the people work on farms or fishing. The main crops are rice, vegetables and fruit. Farm machinery, chemicals and cement are made in North Korea's factories.

Some people in North Korea follow the teachings of an ancient Chinese philosopher called Confucius. He taught that everyone should respect people who are older.

On special occasions people wear colourful costumes and perform dances from North Korea's past.

All school children are members of the Young Pioneers, which is like the scouts. They learn about the country's communist political system.

DID YOU KNOW?

North Korea and South Korea were formed as two separate countries in 1945, after World War II.

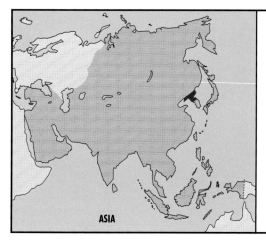

ASIA

FACT FILE

PEOPLE	North Koreans
POPULATION	23.5 million
MAIN LANGUAGE	Korean
CAPITAL CITY	Pyongyang
MONEY	North Korean won
HIGHEST MOUNTAIN	Mount Paektu – 2744 m
LONGEST RIVER	River Yalu – 790 km

Northern Ireland

See also: United Kingdom

Northern Ireland is one of the four main parts of the United Kingdom. It is on the island of Ireland. There are areas of hills with mountains that drop steeply into the sea.

Living and working

The mild and wet weather helps the grass to grow for the dairy cattle. Some farmers grow a crop called flax that is made into linen cloth. There are many factories making electrical goods, aircraft and ships.

There has been violence in Northern Ireland for over 30 years. It is caused by fighting over who should govern Northern Ireland. Some groups want a United Ireland, and some want to be governed by the United Kingdom.

Carrickfergus Castle is one of many ancient castles on the Northern Irish coast.

DID YOU KNOW?

The Giant's Causeway is a stretch of stones that looks like steps. It reaches out into the sea, at Antrim in Northern Ireland. Local legends say that it was built by a giant. The truth is less exciting. It was formed by a flow of hot rock, which cooled and set into oddly-shaped columns.

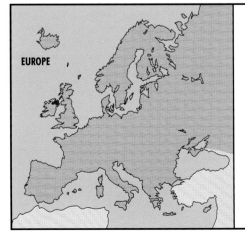

EUROPE

FACT FILE

PEOPLE	British, Irish
POPULATION	1.6 million
MAIN LANGUAGE	English
CAPITAL CITY	Belfast
MONEY	Pound sterling
HIGHEST MOUNTAIN	Slieve Donard – 852 m
LONGEST RIVER	River Bann – 122 km

Norway

See also: Arctic, Europe, Vikings

Norway is a country in north-west Europe. There are mountains and high flatlands. The coast has a wavy edge, with long, narrow bays called fjords that push inland. Inland, winters are cold and summers are hot. It is warmer on the coast.

Living and working

Most Norwegians live in cities and towns. Under the North Sea off Norway, there is gas and oil in the rocks. They are brought to shore in special pipes and sold to other countries. This has made Norway a very rich country.

The people in Norway catch and eat fish called herring. They serve it in many different ways. Lingonberries that grow during the short summers are made into jam. Norway was part of the ancient Viking kingdom. Crafts, including cloth and metalwork, still use Viking designs.

These brightly painted houses in the town of Bergen were built for merchants about 500 years ago.

DID YOU KNOW?

Bronze Age rock carvings in Norway show the world's first skiers. The carvings are over 4000 years old.

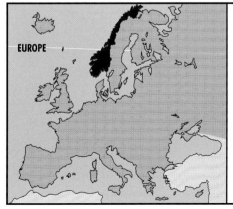

EUROPE

FACT FILE

PEOPLE....................... Norwegians

POPULATION............... 4.3 million

MAIN LANGUAGE......... Norwegian

CAPITAL CITY.............. Oslo

MONEY....................... Krone

HIGHEST MOUNTAIN... Galdhøpiggen – 2469 m

LONGEST RIVER........... Glåmma – 610 km

Numbers

See also: Computer, Money

People use numbers to count things. They use them to answer the question, 'How many?' They use the special symbols called numerals to write the answer down. People who study numbers are called mathematicians.

The first numbers

One of the earliest ways of counting, and the one most people use today, is called decimal. It is based on the number ten. Ten was chosen because it is easy to count on your fingers. Two lots of fingers and two thumbs make ten.

The big numbers on these basketball players shirts help to identify the players.

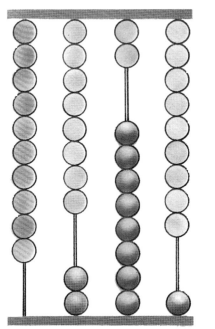

The abacus is an ancient Chinese counting machine. It is still used in some countries. This abacus shows the number 281.

Why are numbers important?

Everyone needs numbers when they want to count things. Numbers are used to count how many people can be safely let into a football match, and then to keep the score. Shopkeepers use numbers to count the things they have to sell, to decide when to order more stock and to work out how much customers owe them.

DID YOU KNOW?

Computers do not use decimal numbers. All the information in a computer is stored using patterns of 0s and 1s. This system is called binary. For example in binary 0 means zero and 1 means one. But two would be written as 10.

Nutrition

See also: Food chain

Nutrition is the food that humans and animals eat to stay alive. Food is needed as fuel to keep the body running and give it the energy it needs. The important parts in food, used by the body, are called nutrients.

DID YOU KNOW?

The energy in food is measured in calories (or joules). The more active a person is, the more calories their body needs for energy.

Healthy eating

A balanced diet contains all the foods a body needs. It means eating the right amounts of the different nutrients. If someone does not have a balanced diet, they become ill. Eating too many 'energy' foods can make a person fat.

About 40 million people each year die of starvation because they don't get enough to eat. Others become ill or die from malnutrition. This means 'bad nutrition'. They die from eating the wrong foods.

Fats Butter, cooking oil and chocolate have a lot of fat. Too much is bad for the body.

Dairy products These provide calcium for healthy bones and teeth.

Starches Bread, pasta and rice are starch food. They give energy.

Meat, beans and fish These give protein to help children grow.

Fruit and vegetables These give fibre, vitamins and minerals that the body needs.

The Healthy Eating Pyramid. To stay healthy, a person should eat most foods from the bottom of the pyramid, some from the middle and least from the top.

Ocean

See also: Water

An ocean is a very big area of water. There are five oceans: the Atlantic, the Antarctic, the Arctic, the Indian and the Pacific. Oceans are much bigger than seas. The Pacific Ocean is the biggest ocean. The Arctic Ocean is the smallest. About three-quarters of the Earth's surface is covered by water.

DID YOU KNOW?

The deepest part in all of the oceans is in the Mariana Trench in the Pacific Ocean. It is over eleven kilometres deep.

Under the water

The bottom of the ocean is called the ocean bed. Some of the ocean bed is flat. There are also underwater mountain ranges. Some of the mountains are active volcanoes. Some islands are the tops of underwater mountains that reach above the surface of the water. The deepest parts of the oceans are called trenches. Water flows around the oceans in patterns called currents. The Gulf Stream is a warm current that flows across the Atlantic Ocean.

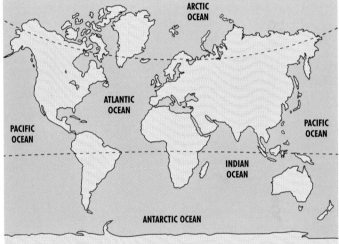

The oceans of the world.

People and oceans

Ships carry goods across the oceans. People fish in the oceans and enjoy sailing and other water sports. People also dump waste in the oceans, causing pollution. Sometimes there are oil spills. Seabirds, fish and other animals can die when an ocean gets polluted.

Large masses of ice called icebergs can break off glaciers in the Arctic and in Antarctica and float out into the oceans.

Octopus

See also: Mollusc, Squid

The octopus is a large mollusc with eight legs called tentacles. It has no bones and no shell. It lives on the sea floor. The octopus protects itself by spraying a fluid called ink at its enemies. The common octopus is found in all warm oceans. The giant octopus is found in the Pacific Ocean.

Octopus families

Each octopus makes its own nest in gravel or in the rocks. This nest is called a lair. The female lays many thousands of eggs inside her lair. She moves water over her eggs to keep them clean for months until they hatch, and never goes out to hunt.

OCTOPUS FACTS

NUMBER OF KINDS	about 50
COLOUR	many different colours
LENGTH	up to 3.5 m with tentacles (7 m across)
WEIGHT	up to 70 kg
STATUS	common
LIFE SPAN	2–3 years
ENEMIES	people

Special skin that changes colour to help the octopus hide

Suckers for holding onto rocks and food

A deep-sea octopus

Siphon to push water out very fast to help the octopus move

The female octopus looks after her eggs until they hatch. These baby Australian octopuses are just hatching.

FOOD

An octopus eats crabs, lobsters and small shellfish. It uses its powerful beak to crush the shells.

Olympic Games

See also: Greece (Ancient)

The Olympic Games is an international sporting competition. People from countries all over the world join in. The games are held every four years.

The first Olympics

The first Olympics were held in Ancient Greece. They were part of a big religious ceremony, which people came to from all over Greece. After the ceremonies, there were sporting events – races, wrestling, boxing and throwing. The men who won got a crown of laurel leaves.

KEY DATES

776 BC..........	The first Olympics were held in Ancient Greece
AD 393.........	The Roman Emperor, Theodosius I, stopped all non-Christian ceremonies, including the Olympics
1896	The first modern Olympics were held in Athens
1916............	The Olympics were cancelled because of World War I
1940, 1944..	The Olympics were cancelled because of World War II

The modern Olympics

The first modern Olympics were held in 1896, in Athens, Greece. It was just a sporting competition, not a religious ceremony. The modern Olympics also include sports such as rifle shooting, as well as races and throwing. Men and women compete. The winner of each event gets a gold medal.

DID YOU KNOW?

There are Summer and Winter Olympics. Between each summer and each winter Olympics there are four years. But there are only two years between summer and winter Olympics. This means there is an Olympics every two years.

The ancient Olympics were shown on some of the vases the people used.

Opera

See also: Drama, Music, Orchestra, Theatre

Opera uses singing, acting and music to tell a story. Usually, the characters in opera sing all of their part of the story. Some operas tell sad stories. Others tell funny ones. The music for an opera is played by an orchestra. Operas are still written today.

This scene is from a famous opera by the German composer, Richard Wagner.

European operas

The first operas were written in Italy 400 years ago. The style spread through Europe and became very popular.

This shows a scene from a Chinese opera. The only scenery is a painted backdrop.

Many famous composers of classical music, including Mozart and Wagner, also wrote operas. In the 1800s short operas, called operettas, with more spoken words, were written and performed. The English composers, Gilbert and Sullivan, wrote many operettas.

Chinese opera

There has been a type of opera in China for many hundreds of years. The stories are usually about adventure or love. There is not much scenery, but the costumes and make-up worn by the actors are very fancy and detailed.

DID YOU KNOW?

Modern musicals such as *Phantom of the Opera* and *West Side Story* are a kind of operetta.

Opossum

See also: Mammal, Marsupial

The opossum is a marsupial mammal that lives in North America and South America. It is related to the marsupial possum of Australia and New Zealand.

Opossum families

Each adult opossum lives in a nest of dead leaves in a hollow tree, under a pile of dead wood or in an old burrow. A female opossum can have 25 babies at a time, but can only feed twelve or thirteen of them in her pouch. The others die.

The live babies stay in the pouch for ten weeks, until they are too big to fit inside. They then come out to live in their mother's nest.

OPOSSUM FACTS

NUMBER OF KINDS	77
COLOUR	black, grey, brown or white
WEIGHT	up to 6 kg
LENGTH	104 cm
STATUS	common
LIFE SPAN	about 2 years
ENEMIES	people

An opossum

Very good ears, for listening for prey in the night time

Long, curly tail for holding onto branches

Strong claws for climbing and digging

When a female opposum goes out hunting, she can carry her young on her back.

FOOD

Some opossums eat fruit and berries. The Virginia opossum of North America eats mostly rodents, but can also kill hens.

Orchestra

See also: Classical music

An orchestra is a large group of musicians playing together. The most common kind of orchestra is made up of stringed, woodwind, brass and percussion instruments. It plays classical music and other music written for these instruments.

The first orchestra

Claudio Monteverdi, a composer who lived in Italy 400 years ago, was the first to write music for an orchestra. Since that time, new instruments have been invented, so orchestras have changed.

Outside Europe, other groups of musicians play different instruments together. In Indonesia, gamelan orchestras play mainly percussion instruments. In Russia, there are balalaika orchestras. They play different sizes of the balalaika, a stringed instrument.

Orchestras today

Today, composers still write for the standard orchestra. There are also composers who add unusual sounds to the orchestra, such as car horns and alarm clocks.

Some modern composers use a computer or an electronic keyboard to copy the different sounds of the instruments in the orchestra. The composer can create the sound of a full orchestra without one being there.

This is how a classical orchestra is usually arranged for a concert.

Ostrich

See also: Africa, Bird

The ostrich is the largest bird in the world. It lives in the grasslands of central and southern Africa. The ostrich cannot fly, but it can run at 60 kph. This is faster than all other African animals except the cheetah. Its eggs are the biggest of any living creature. The kick of a male ostrich is so powerful that it can badly injure a lion.

Ostrich families

A female ostrich is called a hen. A male ostrich makes several nests, called scrapes, in the soil. His favourite female chooses one scrape and lays her eggs in it. Other females lay eggs in the same nest. Chicks from several nests form a large flock that is guarded by only one or two adults.

OSTRICH FACTS

NUMBER OF KINDS	1
COLOUR	black/brown, white and pink
HEIGHT	up to 2.75 m
WEIGHT	up to 150 kg
STATUS	some endangered
LIFE SPAN	up to 40 years
ENEMIES	hyenas, jackals, people

Long neck with stretchy skin for swallowing big pieces of food

Ostriches are hunted for their long, fluffy feathers

Very strong feet and legs for running and kicking

An ostrich

An adult ostrich watching over the eggs. Only the male and his favourite hen look after the eggs.

FOOD

An ostrich eats plants, shoots, leaves, flowers, seeds and insects. It also swallows grit and small stones to help it digest its food.

Otter

See also: Mammal

The otter is a playful mammal which spends most of its time in water. Most kinds live in rivers, but the sea otter lives in the Pacific Ocean.

Otter families

A male otter is called a dog. A baby otter is called a cub. A river otter's home is a burrow called a holt. Each dog otter has two or more females in his large territory. Each female feeds and teaches her own two or three cubs.

The male and female sea otters live in separate groups for most of the year. Female sea otters only have one cub at a time. The sea otter doesn't have a home. It ties itself to a piece of seaweed before going to sleep.

OTTER FACTS

NUMBER OF KINDS	6
COLOUR	brown
LENGTH	up to 1.2 m
WEIGHT	up to 45 kg
STATUS	some threatened
LIFE SPAN	up to 20 years
ENEMIES	people

Oily, waterproof fur for keeping dry and warm

Strong jaws and sharp teeth for catching fish

Strong tail for steering while swimming and fighting

Webbed feet for swimming

An Asian short-clawed otter

This female sea otter is floating on her back while her baby sleeps on her tummy.

FOOD

A river otter eats mostly fish, particularly eels. They also eat frogs, crayfish and water insects. The sea otter eats abalone, a kind of shellfish.

Owl

See also: Bird

The owl is a bird of prey which hunts at night. There are many different kinds of owl that live all over the world.

Owl families

The male and female owl make a nest in a tree or a farm building. The female owl lays one egg every few days. She may lay up to seven eggs. The female sits on the eggs, while the male brings her food.

A baby owl is called an owlet. When the owlets are a few days old, the female leaves the nest to hunt for food. After a few weeks the owlets leave home.

OWL FACTS

NUMBER OF KINDS	133
COLOUR	usually brown or brown and white
LENGTH	up to 72 cm
WEIGHT	up to 800 g
STATUS	common
LIFE SPAN	up to 18 years
ENEMIES	eagles, buzzards, people

Large and powerful eyes help it to see in the dark

Soft feathers for making less noise when flying

Small, sharp bill for ripping meat

A barn owl

Strong claws and feet for holding food and fighting

A female great-horned owl looks after her owlets in a nest in a tree.

FOOD

An owl catches mice, rats and voles by dropping down from the sky and grabbing them in its strong claws. Owls that eat fish have no feathers on their legs.

Oxygen

See also: Air, Lung, Plant

Oxygen is one of the gases in the air. It is the part of the air that our bodies use. Without oxygen, humans and animals would die.

Human beings cannot take oxygen out of water like fish can. This diver has a tank of oxygen. He breathes it in through a mouthpiece.

Plants and oxygen

About one-fifth of fresh air is oxygen. All humans and animals use oxygen when they breathe. They then breathe out a gas called carbon dioxide. In the sunlight, plants take carbon dioxide from the air and give out oxygen. If there were no plants, oxygen would get used up.

Using oxygen

Fires can only burn when they have oxygen. One way to put out a fire is to make sure there is no oxygen. Covering a fire with foam or a special fire-blanket does this.

Oxygen also helps metals to corrode. If you keep oxygen away from metals they can't corrode. Covering metals with paint stops them corroding because paint keeps the oxygen out.

Pure oxygen can make fire burn very strongly. In welding torches, oxygen is used to make a flame that is hot enough to melt metal.

DID YOU KNOW?

If oxygen is cooled down it will turn into a liquid. Rocket engines use liquid oxygen to burn their fuel.

Painting

See also: Art

Painters make marks on a
surface using paints, such as oil
paints or water-colours. This
surface can be paper, wood,
canvas, plaster, stone or even
a person.

The first painting

Painting is one of the very oldest kinds
of art. The earliest paintings were made
by prehistoric people on cave walls.
Many of these are hunting scenes. They
were probably done to bring good
luck to the hunters or to record a
successful hunt.

Over the centuries, painting became
important. Powerful people would
employ artists to paint pictures of them,
their families or their possessions.
Painters would also make religious
paintings, or paint the local area.

Leonardo da Vinci (1452–1519)

Leonardo da Vinci was born in Italy.
He was a painter, sculptor, architect,
engineer and scientist. His famous portrait
Mona Lisa (above) is one of the most
popular paintings in the world. Another of
his famous paintings is *The Last Supper*, a
large picture of Jesus and the Apostles,
which he painted onto the wall of an
Italian monastery.

DID YOU KNOW?

Some paintings made in the last 100 years
are not pictures of people, places and
things. Instead, they try to show ideas or
feelings using colours, patterns and shapes.
This kind of painting is called abstract.

*The tribespeople of Papua New
Guinea paint their bodies.*

Pakistan

See also: Asia

Pakistan is a country in the south of Asia. There are high mountains over half the country. The River Indus flows through the lowlands. The weather is hot and wet in summer. It is warm and dry in winter.

DID YOU KNOW?

Pakistan became an independent country in 1947, at the same time as India.

Living and working

Farmers grow rice, wheat and vegetables. They cut flat fields into the steep hillsides to make more land for farming. In the cities there are factories where clothes, rugs and foods are made.

Most Pakistanis are followers of the religion of Islam. They celebrate Islamic festivals. A favourite food is rice and hot curries.

This fabric shop sells colourful and decorated cloth that can be used to make clothing. The most expensive is silk with threads of real gold.

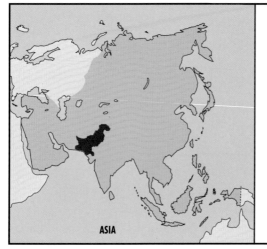

ASIA

FACT FILE

PEOPLE	Pakistanis
POPULATION	136.6 million
MAIN LANGUAGE	Urdu
CAPITAL CITY	Islamabad
BIGGEST CITY	Karachi
MONEY	Rupee
HIGHEST MOUNTAIN	K2 – 8611 m
LONGEST RIVER	River Indus – 3100 km

Panama

See also: North America, Waterway

Panama is a small country in Central America. It is on a narrow strip of land with the Atlantic Ocean on one side and the Pacific Ocean on the other. There are mountains over most of the country. The weather is mostly hot and rainy. Rainforests cover about half of Panama.

Living and working

Most people work in factories or work with the ships that pass through the Panama Canal. About one-third of the people make a living by farming. Farmers grow rice, maize, beans, bananas and coffee.

People celebrate Christian festivals and saints' days. There are also local native Indian festivals. In one native Indian festival, young men throw light, soft logs from the balsa trees at each other.

The Panama Canal opened in 1914. Ships can sail through the Panama Canal between the Atlantic Ocean and the Pacific Ocean.

DID YOU KNOW?

It takes up to nine hours for a large ship to go through the Panama Canal. Going through the canal cuts 12,000 km off the old journey around southern tip of South America.

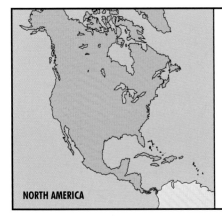

NORTH AMERICA

FACT FILE

PEOPLE	Panamanians
POPULATION	2.6 million
MAIN LANGUAGE	Spanish
CAPITAL CITY	Panama City
MONEY	Balboa
HIGHEST MOUNTAIN	Volcan Baru – 3475 m
LONGEST RIVER	River Tuira – 170 km

Panda

See also: Endangered species, Mammal

A panda is a furry mammal. There are two kinds of panda. The giant panda looks a bit like a black and white bear. The smaller, red panda looks a bit like a chubby cat. There are only about 1000 pandas left in the world. They all live in one part of China.

Panda families

Giant panda babies are called cubs. When they are born they are tiny, weighing only about 100 g. They leave their mothers at a year old. Adult giant pandas live most of their lives on their own, pushing through the forest, climbing trees and eating.

PANDA FACTS

NUMBER OF KINDS	2
WEIGHT........	giant panda – 100–104 kg
	red panda – 3–5 kg
LENGTH........	giant panda – 1.5 m
	red panda – 0.5 m
LIFE SPAN......	up to 20 years
STATUS.........	endangered
ENEMIES........	people

Thumb-type bones on paws for holding bamboo shoots

A young giant panda

Thick, waterproof fur for keeping warm and dry

All pandas only like to eat bamboo shoots.

FOOD

Pandas eat a kind of tall grass called bamboo. Giant pandas have to eat for at least 12 hours a day, to stay alive.

Papua New Guinea

See also: Australasia

Papua New Guinea is a country in Australasia. It includes the eastern half of the island of New Guinea, as well as 600 small islands. Mountains with thick forest are in the centre. The climate is hot and it rains a lot.

Living and working

Most Papuans live in the countryside. Farmers grow bananas and root crops, and raise pigs. There are gold, copper and silver mines. Timber, fish, coffee, coconuts and cocoa are sold to other countries.

Fish and other seafood are served with yams, sweet potatoes or *taros*. This is the soft insides of the sago palm. Meat, vegetables and herbs are baked in an underground oven, called a *mumu*. Many of the islands are famous for their dances. New Ireland island has 50 different dances.

This house is made of wood and built on stilts to keep it dry. It is home for an entire village.

DID YOU KNOW?

The bird on the Papuan flag is called a kumul. It is a type of bird of paradise.

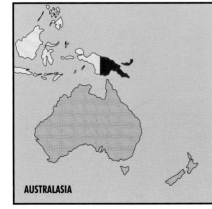
AUSTRALASIA

FACT FILE

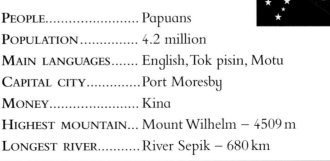

PEOPLE	Papuans
POPULATION	4.2 million
MAIN LANGUAGES	English, Tok pisin, Motu
CAPITAL CITY	Port Moresby
MONEY	Kina
HIGHEST MOUNTAIN	Mount Wilhelm — 4509 m
LONGEST RIVER	River Sepik — 680 km

Parrot

See also: Bird

A parrot is a brightly coloured bird that lives in warm countries all around the world. Most kinds live in forests, but a few live in the desert.

Parrot families

Parrots live together in large flocks. The female usually makes the nest in a tree, partly from wood. She lays up to six eggs and sits on them, while the male brings her food. The chicks stay with their parents until they leave to have chicks of their own.

FOOD

Parrots have specially shaped big beaks for eating fruit and seeds. Some parrots eat flowers.

PARROT FACTS

NUMBER OF KINDS	about 320
COLOUR	many colours
LENGTH	up to 1 m
WEIGHT	up to 2.5 kg
STATUS	rare in wild
LIFE SPAN	about 40 years
ENEMIES	eagles, falcons, people

Large beak for cracking nuts and seeds, and for holding on when climbing.

Strong feet for climbing and holding on

Long tail to help balance

This Australian ring-necked parrot has just landed by its nest in a tree hollow.

A scarlet macaw parrot

Penguin

See also: Antarctica, Bird

The penguin is a bird, but it cannot fly. It can swim very well, and can stay under water for several minutes. There are eighteen kinds of penguin and they mostly live in and around the cold Antarctic.

Penguin families

Penguins come onto land to breed, after months of eating at sea. The male arrives first. He finds a place to nest and waits for the female. Then they make a nest of rocks. The female lays one egg. The parents take turns in looking after the egg and then, the chick.

Baby penguins are very fluffy. This helps to keep them warm. When the chicks are young a few adult penguins look after lots of babies together. A group of penguins is called a rookery.

PENGUIN FACTS

NUMBER OF KINDS	18
COLOUR	black and white
HEIGHT	up to 112 cm
WEIGHT	up to 40 kg
STATUS	common
LIFE SPAN	up to 20 years
ENEMIES	sea leopards, people

An emperor penguin

Thick fat under the skin to keep body heat in

Stiff wings like flippers for swimming

Long, waterproof feathers for warmth

Triangular tail for steering while swimming

FOOD

A penguin catches its food under water. It eats krill, crabs, fish and squid.

Emperor penguin parents take turns looking after the chick while the other parent goes to sea to feed.

Peninsula

See also: Coast

A peninsula is a narrow piece of land that sticks out into the sea like a finger. It has water almost all the way around it, except where it is joined to the mainland. Some peninsulas are very big. Most of the country of Italy is a long peninsula that juts out into the Mediterranean Sea.
A peninsula can also be much smaller, less than a kilometre long.

How a peninsula is made
Most peninsulas are areas with hard rock or mountains. The sea wears away the soft land but leaves the hard bits. It takes tens of thousands of years to do this.

Peninsulas and people
Some people who live on peninsulas make a living by fishing. They are also popular places for holidays by the sea, because of the coastline.

The Baja Peninsula in Mexico has many holiday resorts.

DID YOU KNOW?
The world's biggest peninsula is Arabia. It is surrounded on three sides by water.

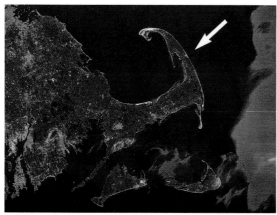

This is a satellite picture of the peninsula called Cape Cod in Massachusetts, USA.

Some World Peninsulas
Scandinavian peninsula... Europe
Iberian peninsula............Europe
Brittany peninsula..........Europe
Yucatan peninsula..........Central America
Kamchatka peninsula......Asia
Alaska peninsula.............North America

Percussion instruments

See also: Music, Musical instruments

Percussion instruments are musical instruments that make a sound when they are hit or shaken. Drums, cymbals gongs, bells, rattles and wood blocks are all kinds of percussion instruments. The very first percussion instruments were people's hands and feet, which they used to make clapping and stamping sounds.

DID YOU KNOW?

The piano is a percussion instrument. When the keys are played, tiny hammers hit tightly stretched wires.

Drummers from the Tutsi tribe from Rwanda in Africa drumming together.

The drum kit is a set of percussion instruments used in rock, pop, jazz and some classical music.

Types of Percussion Instruments

Drums: These are made by stretching something across a hollow box, then hitting it with a stick or the hands.

Found percussion instruments: These are natural objects which have their own special sounds. For example, a living tree can be hit with a stick, or two rocks can be tapped together.

Metal percussion instruments: These include gongs, cymbals, bells and tambourines. Some are played with sticks or beaters while others are played by shaking or crashing them together.

Wooden percussion instruments: These are often hollow wooden boxes which make a sharp clicking or booming sound when they are hit.

Peru

See also: Incas, South America

Peru is a country in the north-west of South America. There is lowland along the coast and the Andes Mountains inland. There is high flat land with Lake Titicaca in the south. Earthquakes and active volcanoes sometimes kill people and make buildings collapse.

Living and working

Farmers grow potatoes, rice and sugar. Some raise sheep, llamas and alpacas. The alpaca has very fine wool. Almost three-quarters of the people live and work in towns and cities.

Most people in Peru are Roman Catholic Christians. They celebrate religious festivals at Easter and on saints' days. Many festivals with dancing, music and masks come from the old Indian cultures of Peru. Music is played on pan pipes and flutes. Some tourists go to see the remains of ancient Inca cities.

This woman from the Quecha tribe in the Andes is weaving belts.

DID YOU KNOW?

The red and white colours in the flag of Peru stand for red and white flamingos.

SOUTH AMERICA

FACT FILE

PEOPLE .... Peruvians

POPULATION .... 23.5 million

MAIN LANGUAGES........ Spanish, Quechua

CAPITAL CITY..............Lima

MONEY....................... New sol

HIGHEST MOUNTAIN ... Huascarán – 6768 m

LONGEST RIVER............River Ucayali – 2300 km

Philippines

See also: Asia

The Philippines is a country in south-east Asia made up of islands. The main islands have mountains and river valleys. The climate is hot. Every year there are heavy rains called monsoons.

Living and working

About half the people live in the countryside. In some villages, the community lives in a wooden 'long house', raised above the ground. Farmers grow rice, sugar cane, corn, pineapples and coconuts. A favourite food in the Philippines is *siopao*. It is a kind of dumpling filled with minced meat.

The Philippines is the only country in Asia where most of the people are Christians. This is because Spanish missionaries came to the Philippines over 450 years ago.

These are women of the Ifugo tribe. Where they live is famous for its terraces for growing rice.

DID YOU KNOW?

Basketball is the most popular sport in the Philippines. There are also two special Filipino games. *Arnis* is a kind of sword-fighting played with wooden sticks. *Sipa* is a game that is a bit like volleyball.

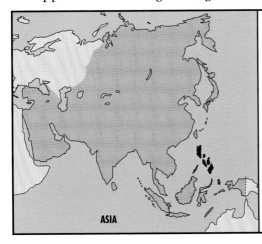

ASIA

FACT FILE

PEOPLE	Filipinos
POPULATION	66.2 million
MAIN LANGUAGES	Pilipino (Tagalog), English
CAPITAL CITY	Manila
MONEY	Philippine peso
HIGHEST MOUNTAIN	Mount Apo – 2954 m
LONGEST RIVER	River Cagayan – 180 km

Photosynthesis

See also: Leaf, Plant

Green plants use the energy of sunlight to make their own food. This is called photosynthesis.

How photosynthesis works

Leaves are a plant's factories for making food. The green stuff in leaves, called chlorophyll, takes in energy from sunlight. The chlorophyll uses carbon dioxide from the air and water from the soil to make sugary food for the plant.

Oxygen is given out into the air during photosynthesis. Only green plants make their own food this way. Plants then provide food for animals. Even animals that do not eat plants feed on animals that do eat plants. Without photosynthesis, animals and people could not survive.

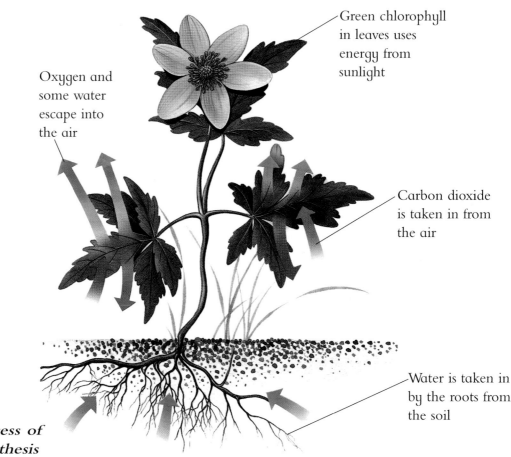

Green chlorophyll in leaves uses energy from sunlight

Oxygen and some water escape into the air

Carbon dioxide is taken in from the air

Water is taken in by the roots from the soil

The process of photosynthesis

Pig

See also: Farming, Mammal

A pig is a mammal. In some countries there are wild pigs, but farmers all over the world keep pigs for food. Bacon, pork, ham and sausages come from pigs. Some kinds of pig are very hairy. Other kinds have smooth pink skin.

Pig families

A male pig is called a boar and a female pig is called a sow. Pig babies are called piglets. Sows on farms can have up to 20 piglets in one litter.

Pigs once lived wild in forests. Now most pigs are kept for food and live in farm buildings or in fields.

PIG FACTS

NUMBER OF	
KINDS..............over 80	
COLOUR......... white, brown, black, red	
WEIGHT..........up to 200 kg	
LENGTH.......... 1.5 m	
STATUS...........common	
LIFE SPAN........ 10 years	
ENEMIES .... wolves, people	

Some pigs are bred to have big, fat bodies, so there is more meat

Floppy ears flap insects away

Teats to feed milk to piglets

A female pig

Turned up snout for searching out food and digging it

This sow has had a litter of seventeen piglets.

FOOD

Pigs are scavengers – this means they will eat just about anything.

Pigeon

See also: Bird

A pigeon is a bird. Many kinds of pigeon live in woods, on cliffs and in towns and cities all around the world. Pigeons make a sound called cooing. Some pigeons are also called doves.

Pigeon families

When they are not nesting, pigeons live together in big groups called flocks. A baby pigeon is called a squab. Each spring the male and female pigeon pick a nesting site and the male collects twigs and stems to weave a nest. The female lays two to four eggs.

After the babies are born the adults feed them on 'pigeon's milk', which they make from digested food.

The strong, wide wings for flying

PIGEON FACTS

NUMBER OF KINDS	255
COLOUR	many colours
WEIGHT	up to 2 kg
LENGTH	up to 80 cm
STATUS	common
LIFE SPAN	up to 15 years
ENEMIES	buzzards, falcons, martens, foxes, badgers, people

A wood pigeon

Long claws on feet for holding on to branches and ledges while sleeping

These Australian crested pigeons walk right into the water to drink.

FOOD

A pigeon eats grain, leaves and fruit. Sometimes large flocks of pigeons feed off crops in farmers' fields. Farmers don't like pigeons.

Planets

See also: Solar system, Sun

Planets are large balls of gas and rock that orbit a star. Nine planets have been discovered in our solar system. The Earth is one of them. The others are Mercury, Venus, Mars, Jupiter, Saturn, Uranus, Neptune and Pluto. Some of the other stars in the sky also have planets orbiting them.

Mercury
58 million km from sun

Venus
108 million km from sun

Earth
150 million km from sun

Mars
228 million km from sun

Jupiter
778 million km
from sun

The nine planets

All nine planets orbit the sun. The planets near to the sun are hottest and those far from the sun are coldest. Some of the nine planets can be seen without a telescope. From the Earth, they look like stars. Uranus, Neptune and Pluto can only be seen with a telescope. People have never landed on another planet yet. Space exploration probes have taken pictures of all nine except Pluto. Space exploration probes have landed on Mars and Venus.

Saturn
1427 million km
from sun

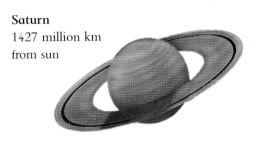

Uranus
2870 million km from sun

Neptune
4500 million km from sun

Pluto
5900 million km from sun

These are the nine planets of our solar system. This shows how their sizes are very different.

DID YOU KNOW?

Someone who studies the objects in space is called an astronomer. The study of space is called astronomy. It is the oldest science.

Plant

See also: Photosynthesis

A plant is a living thing that grows and stays in one place. Plants grow all over the world. A person who studies plants is called a botanist.

PLANT FACTS

NUMBER OF KINDS	over 260,000
HEIGHT	microscopic up to 88 m
LIFE SPAN	up to 5000 years
ENEMIES	bacteria, insects, people

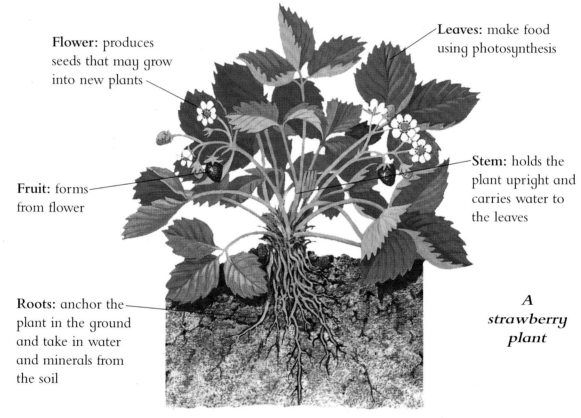

Flower: produces seeds that may grow into new plants

Leaves: make food using photosynthesis

Fruit: forms from flower

Stem: holds the plant upright and carries water to the leaves

Roots: anchor the plant in the ground and take in water and minerals from the soil

A strawberry plant

The life of a plant

Most plants grow from seeds made in the flowers of the parent plant. Some plants, such as ferns and mosses, grow from spores. Each kind of plant needs water, sunlight and nutrients from the soil to grow. Different kinds of plants grow best in different kinds of places – forests, deserts, fields and even in the oceans.

People and plants

Plants provide people with food, medicines and many useful materials. Rubber, cotton, paper, rope and wood are just some of the materials that come from plants. Plants also give all animals oxygen to breathe. Plants take the carbon dioxide out of the air and put oxygen into the air.

Plastic

See also: Heat, Mining

Plastic is a man-made material that can be formed into many shapes. Most plastic is made from chemicals in petroleum oil. Some plastics are hard. Some plastics are bendy. Most plastics are lighter than metals.

Making things from plastic

Plastics are easy to shape by moulding. A mould is an empty shape that a liquid can be poured into. Plastic is melted and pushed or sucked into moulds. When it cools down it hardens and keeps the shape of the mould. Plastic can also be used to make thread and fibres to make cloth. Nylon, rayon and polyester are plastics used in this way.

PVC
polystyrene
polycarbonate
polythene
nylon

Different types of plastic are used to make different things.

Recycling plastic

Plastic doesn't rot or corrode. Because of this, plastic objects in rubbish stay in the ground at the tips.

Supplies of oil are running out, so to save oil some plastics can be melted down and used again. Plastic drinks bottles and other containers can be treated in this way. This is called recycling.

DID YOU KNOW?

One of the first kinds of plastic used was invented in 1908 by a Belgian who moved to the United States. His name was Leo Hendrik Baekeland. The plastic he invented was called Bakelite. It broke easily, so it is no longer used.

Platypus

See also: Australia, Mammal

A platypus is one of the strangest of all mammals. It has a bill like a bird and lays eggs, but it has fur like most mammals. It lives only in Australia.

Platypus families

Each platypus digs a tunnel in the river bank and lives on its own. Every autumn the female platypus digs a long tunnel and lays two or three eggs in it. She holds the eggs with her tail to keep them warm. After the eggs hatch, their mother keeps the babies in her tunnel until they are about four to five months old. Like other mammals, she feeds them on milk.

PLATYPUS FACTS

NUMBER OF KINDS	1
COLOUR	brown
LENGTH	about 60 cm
WEIGHT	about 2 kg
STATUS	rare
LIFE SPAN	not known
ENEMIES	pollution in water

Thick, waterproof fur for swimming

A platypus

Nostrils, eyes and ears close to keep water out when swimming

Wide, webbed front paws for fast swimming and claws for digging

Bill for picking up food from the bottom of rivers and streams

This platypus is digging food from a riverbed.

FOOD

A platypus eats insect larvae, water snails and crayfish. It collects food from the river surface and floor in its cheek pouches. When the pouches are full it brings the food to the surface to eat.

Poetry

See also: Literature

Poetry uses words in verses to tell a story or describe feelings. It is a kind of literature. A piece of poetry is called a poem. Someone who writes poetry is called a poet.

The first poems

The first poems were really songs. The words were sung or recited to music. About 2500 years ago, people started writing and reciting verses without music, but they still kept the rhythms and musical sounds. Many different cultures all over the world have poetry of some kind.

Henry Wadsworth Longfellow (1807–82)

Longfellow was an American poet who helped to make poetry popular. Most of Longfellow's poems were quite long and told stories. His most famous poem is *Hiawatha*. It is a very long poem about a Native American chief. The poem tries to use the rhythms of Native American music and dances.

DID YOU KNOW?

Poetry can tell a story or it can describe the poet's feelings. Characters can be used in the poem to tell the story.

A.A. Milne (1882–1956)

A.A. Milne is famous for the poems and stories he wrote for his son, Christoper Robin. He used Christopher Robin and his toys in his writing. His two books of poetry are called *When We Were Very Young* and *Now We are Six*.

Christoper Robin Milne and his teddy bear, Pooh, with his father.

Kinds of poetry

Since the first poems, different kinds of poetry have been written. Some have lines that rhyme. Most poetry has a rhythm made by strong and weak sounds. This kind of rhythm is called metre.

Poland

See also: Europe

Poland is a country in central Europe. It is mostly lowlands with hills. There are mountains in the south. The only coast is in the north. Summers are warm and winters are cold.

Living and working

Over half the people in Poland live in cities and large towns. Some people work in mines digging out coal, copper, silver, lead, zinc and sulphur. Others make things like ships and machinery. These are sold to other countries. Farmers grow grains, potatoes, sugar beet and fruits, and some raise cattle and pigs.

The people of Poland have many traditional foods. Pancakes and rich cream cakes are favourites. So are thin pork sausages, called *kabanosy*. These are cooked in a creamy sauce.

Traditional national costume is sometimes worn at Poland's many folksong festivals.

DID YOU KNOW?

On 23 June every year a Midsummer Night Festival is held in Warsaw. It is famous for the candles decorated with flowers that are floated down the river.

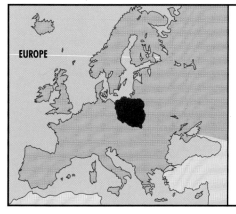

EUROPE

FACT FILE

PEOPLE	Polish, Poles
POPULATION	38.3 million
MAIN LANGUAGE	Polish
CAPITAL CITY	Warsaw
MONEY	Zloty
HIGHEST MOUNTAIN	Rysy – 2499 m
LONGEST RIVER	River Wista – 1115 km

Pollution

See also: Water cycle

Pollution is when something, like air or water is made dirty or damaged. It can be caused by spilling or dumping waste. It can look bad, smell awful, sound noisy or be unhealthy. It can also kill and damage plants, wildlife and even people.

Kinds of Pollution

Air pollution: This comes from car and truck exhausts, and factories.

Sea pollution: This is caused by accidents to oil tankers and other ships, things being dumped overboard, and sewage and chemicals being pumped to the sea from the land.

Water pollution: This is caused when rain washes chemicals used on farms into streams and rivers. Some factories dump waste liquids into streams and rivers.

Litter: Rubbish is often dumped in the streets, in water and in buildings.

Noise pollution: This can be caused by the engines in lorries or aircraft. Other loud noises also add to noise pollution.

Light pollution: Some towns and cities are so bright that it is impossible to see many stars in the sky.

In 1989 an oil tanker ran onto land in Alaska, USA and caused very bad damage. The oil polluted the water and the shore. It killed animals and plant life.

These trees in Poland have been killed by acid rain. Acid rain is caused when pollution in the air makes rainwater bad.

Pop music

See also: Music, Musical instruments

'Pop music' is short for popular music. It means any kind of music which is created for as many people as possible to hear and enjoy. Pop music is usually lively, with catchy tunes and strong rhythms.

The first pop music

Popular music has changed many times over the centuries. The first pop music in English-speaking countries was the ballads sung in taverns, and funny or romantic songs sung in theatres and music halls. Since the 1950s, pop music has changed as new ideas and fashions have come into the music. African-American music from the USA, various kinds of dance music and many other styles have spread around the world. Pop music today is often music with simple rhythms, melodies and words which are easy for listeners to remember.

Normally, pop songs are less than four minutes long. The music is usually performed on electrically amplified instruments with one or more people singing.

Bill Haley (1927–81)

One of the earliest performers of modern pop music was the composer, bandleader, singer and guitarist Bill Haley. He recorded a song called 'Rock Around the Clock' in 1956 with his group, the Comets. The song was about dancing all night long. It was based on African-American music. Haley's group played with a fast beat, using a drum kit and electric guitars. This style called 'rock and roll' spread very quickly.

This pop group, Hanson, is made up of three brothers.

Porcupine

See also: Mammal

A porcupine is a mammal with a coat of sharp spines, called quills. There are two main kinds of porcupine. The African porcupine lives on the ground, and the North American porcupine climbs trees.

Porcupine families

Female African porcupines have two litters a year of two–three babies. The female North American porcupine only has one litter with one baby. In both, the male porcupine doesn't help care for the babies. African and North American porcupine mothers feed their babies on milk for a few weeks before they start feeding themselves.

PORCUPINE FACTS

NUMBER OF KINDS	22
COLOUR	brown or black
WEIGHT	up to 27 kg
LENGTH	up to 80 cm
STATUS	common
LIFE SPAN	up to 15 years
ENEMIES	African – leopards, lions, people North American – pine martens, people

An African porcupine

Long, sharp spines help keep enemies away

Hairless pads on front paws for holding food

Sharp claws for gripping and climbing

It is unusual to see porcupines during the day.

FOOD

Both types of porcupine eat at night. African porcupines eat roots. The North American tree-climbing porcupine likes to eat young leaves and tree bark. Porcupines use their front paws to hold their food while they nibble.

Port

See also: Bay, Coast, Ship

A port is a place on or near land where ships can tie up or drop anchor until they are ready to sail again. The place in a port where ships tie up is called the docks.

Types of port

Some ports are mainly for ships that carry passengers. Most of these are ferry ports. There are also ports for cargo. Ports for cargo ships need cranes, conveyor belts and pipelines to handle the goods.

A port needs to be sheltered from big waves. This can be a harbour in a bay, or where a river comes out to sea. The water must be deep enough for the ships. Some ports have big gates to keep the water in when the tide goes out. These are called lock gates.

Boats going to the United States enter through the port of New York, passing the famous Statue of Liberty.

In ports like Rotterdam in the Netherlands, cargo comes in huge containers that are lifted by cranes from the ship onto the lorries on the docks.

People and ports

Some people in a port build and repair ships. Dock workers, customs officers, lorry drivers and others also work in ports. Many of the world's biggest coastal cities have ports. It is because goods come in and out through the port that those cities have become so big.

DID YOU KNOW?

More ships come and go from the port of Rotterdam in the Netherlands than any other port in the world. Rotterdam is a city where the River Rhine enters the North Sea.

Portugal

See also: Europe

Portugal is a country in the southwest of Europe. There are mountains to the north. In the centre the land is flat and dry. The far south has hot summers. Winters are mild.

Living and working

Many people in Portugal live in villages. In the south, lots of houses are painted white, to reflect the sunlight and keep cool. Cork from trees, and tinned fish are sold to other countries. Clothes, shoes and paper are made in factories. There are farms where grains, olives and grapes are grown. Sheep, cattle and pigs are kept.

Salt cod is the national dish. This is codfish that has been salted and dried. It is served with salad, potatoes and olive oil.

Traditional songs are popular. Each town has its own Christian saint's day festival.

Local folk dances are often performed to accordian music.

DID YOU KNOW?

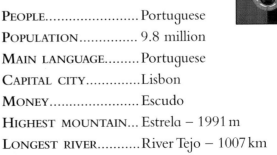

Portugal is famous for its explorers. Europe's first school of astronomy and navigation was opened in Portugal in the 1435.

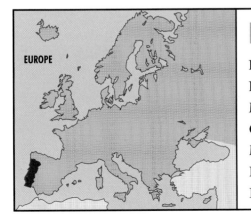

EUROPE

FACT FILE

PEOPLE	Portuguese
POPULATION	9.8 million
MAIN LANGUAGE	Portuguese
CAPITAL CITY	Lisbon
MONEY	Escudo
HIGHEST MOUNTAIN	Estrela – 1991 m
LONGEST RIVER	River Tejo – 1007 km

Praying mantis

See also: Insect, Invertebrate

The praying mantis is an insect. It has a long thin body about the size of an adult finger. When it hunts it holds its strong front legs up in front of its head, as if it is praying. It lives in many warm countries.

How the praying mantis lives

The male praying mantis is smaller than the female. After they mate, the female often eats the male. The female lays her eggs on a plant. The eggs hatch into live insects.

PRAYING MANTIS FACTS

NUMBER OF KINDS	over 2000
COLOUR	green or brown
LENGTH	up to 20 cm
STATUS	becoming rare
ENEMIES	birds, people

Feelers and eyes to smell and see

Shape and colouring for hiding from enemies and food

A praying mantis

Strong front legs with spines to grab food and stop it from wriggling free

FOOD

When the praying mantis hunts it will sit perfectly still. Its powerful front legs are ready for an insect to come close. Then it will quickly grab the insect and eat it alive.

These young praying mantis have just hatched live from their eggs.